Compliance for Green IT

A Pocket Guide

Compliance for Green IT

A Pocket Guide

ALAN CALDER

IT Governance Publishing

Every possible effort has been made to ensure that the information contained in this book is accurate at the time of going to press, and the publishers and the author cannot accept responsibility for any errors or omissions, however caused. No responsibility for loss or damage occasioned to any person acting, or refraining from action, as a result of the material in this publication can be accepted by the publisher or the author.

Apart from any fair dealing for the purposes of research or private study, or criticism or review, as permitted under the Copyright, Designs and Patents Act 1988, this publication may only be reproduced, stored or transmitted, in any form, or by any means, with the prior permission in writing of the publisher or, in the case of reprographic reproduction, in accordance with the terms of licences issued by the Copyright Licensing Agency. Enquiries concerning reproduction outside those terms should be sent to the publishers at the following address:

IT Governance Publishing
IT Governance Limited
Unit 3, Clive Court
Bartholomew's Walk
Cambridgeshire Business Park
Ely
Cambridgeshire
CB7 4EH
United Kingdom

www.itgovernance.co.uk

© Alan Calder 2009
The author has asserted the rights of the author under the Copyright, Designs and Patents Act, 1988, to be identified as the author of this work.

First published in the United Kingdom in 2009
by IT Governance Publishing.

ISBN 978-1-84928-000-6

FOREWORD

Green IT[1] will be a critical component of organisational IT and compliance strategies from 2009 onwards.

There is a range of views about what, exactly, 'Green IT' actually is. At the heart of the debate[2] about the environmental role of IT, there is usually an acknowledgement that the world's information and communications technologies consume a growing amount of power and have a measurably significant carbon footprint.

Regardless of one's individual position or the reality of the argument, there are a number of aspects of climate change – such as the outcomes of the G8 meetings, the United Nations Framework Convention on Climate Change (UNFCCC), Kyoto meetings and the general growth of environmentalism among the public at large – about which individual businesses can do nothing.

Inevitably, this more active environmentalism is increasingly translating into climate-related regulation. Organisations need to have an awareness and understanding of the relevant regulations and legislation so that they can ensure that they take appropriate compliance action.

There are many thousands of environmentally related laws and regulations, only a few of which are of direct importance to the IT professional. It is important that the regulations that are discussed here – the ones that are of most significance in the management of Green IT – are tackled in the context of broader environmental compliance activities.

---

[1] Throughout this report, the term 'IT' (Information Technology) has been used rather than 'ICT' (Information and Communication Technology). The two terms are synonymous, ICT being the preferred acronym in education and government.
[2] See *The Green Agenda: A Business Guide* www.itgovernance.co.uk/products/2202 for an executive overview of the components of this debate.

Regulations that are relevant to the IT sector include carbon trading and carbon cap-and-trade schemes, which are used in a voluntary or mandatory capacity to reduce CO_2 emissions and offset the impact of the environmental damage caused elsewhere. IT is a significant consumer of power and these schemes, while still very much in their infancy, are of growing importance and relevance for the IT organisation. This pocket guide provides a useful introduction to, and overview of, these schemes.

Apart from carbon trading schemes, organisations are increasingly exposed to regulations around the disposal of waste, particularly electronic waste and, again, these regulations have a specific impact on the IT organisation.

This pocket guide is not a legal compliance manual; organisations should refer to the actual legislation or regulations and take advice from a suitably qualified professional on all issues arising from their obligations to comply with environmental legislation.

ABOUT THE AUTHOR

Alan Calder is a leading author on information security and IT governance issues. He is Chief Executive of IT Governance Limited, the one-stop shop for books, tools, training and consultancy on Governance, Risk Management and Compliance. He is also Chairman of the Board of Directors of CEME, a public–private sector skills partnership.

Alan is an international authority on IT governance and, with Steve Moir, originated the innovative Calder-Moir IT Governance Framework. He is also an international expert on ISO27001 (formerly BS7799), the international security standard, about which he wrote with colleague Steve Watkins the definitive compliance guide, *IT Governance: A Manager's Guide to Data Security and BS7799/ISO17799*. This work is based on his experience of leading the world's first successful implementation of BS7799 (with the 4th edition published in May 2008) and is the basis for the UK Open University's postgraduate course on information security.

Other books written by Alan include *The Case for ISO27001*, *Nine Steps to Success: An ISO 27001 Implementation Overview*, *IT Governance: Guidelines for Directors*, *IT Governance Today: A Practitioner's Handbook* and *IT Regulatory Compliance in the UK*.

Alan is a frequent media commentator on information security and IT governance issues, and has contributed articles and expert comment to a wide range of trade, national and online news outlets.

Alan was previously CEO of Wide Learning, a supplier of e-learning; of Focus Central London, a training and enterprise council; and of Business Link London City Partners, a government agency focused on helping growing businesses to develop. He was a member of the Information Age Competitiveness Working Group of the UK Government's Department of Trade and Industry, and was until recently a member of the DNV Certification Services Certification Committee, which certifies compliance with international standards including ISO27001.

ACKNOWLEDGEMENTS

Much of the original content of this pocket guide is drawn from the IT Governance Best Practice Report on the subject of Green IT, which was developed by our in-house research and analysis team and published towards the end of 2008. *Green IT – Reality, Benefits and Best Practices*[3] provides comprehensive, current guidance for organisations that are addressing the challenge of greening their IT operations. This pocket guide, on the other hand, is designed as a specific guide for company directors and executives to the growing range of regulatory requirements that, driven by the Green Agenda, are impacting businesses and IT organisations everywhere.

We are grateful to the European Communities for allowing us to reproduce the WEEE symbol for illustration purposes from Directive 2002/96/EC, http://eur-lex.europa.eu, © European Communities, 1998–2009 as Figure 1 and for allowing us to reproduce the photograph *http://ec.europa.eu/avservices/photo/photo_search_en.cfm?key word=energy+efficiency&videoref* © European Communities, 1995–2009 as Figure 3.

We are also grateful to ENERGY STAR for permission to use their logo in Figure 2.

---

[3] Read about and purchase this report from www.itgovernance.co.uk/products/1933.

CONTENTS

Contents

INTRODUCTION

The growth of environmentalism has meant that there is, in the world at large, a greater awareness of environmental issues and, increasingly, a social drive to:

1. increase energy efficiency
2. increase the proportion of energy generated from sustainable sources
3. reduce the environmental impact of noxious chemicals.

The Kyoto Protocol commits participating countries to reducing their CO_2 emissions. Under the treaty, countries must meet their reduction targets through national regulatory and fiscal measures. The Kyoto Protocol also provides an additional means of meeting their targets by way of market-based mechanisms. Carbon trading has grown out of this.

It is not just those countries that have signed up to the Kyoto agreement who are involved in these measures. For example, China has adopted RoHS and ENERGY STAR. The US is also starting to adopt carbon trading initiatives in the form of auctions at a state, rather than federal level.

Legislative and fiscal initiatives

Many, but not all, of these green initiatives are government-led and usually result in some sort of compromise between the desire to be seen to be meeting environmental targets without at the same time damaging the country's economic growth. Some green initiatives have proved to be more successful than others.

Some legislation and standards, such as RoHS and ENERGY STAR, have been initiated in one country with other versions of the same initiative being adopted in other countries. Other initiatives are more country-restricted.

Accredited certification

International standards, such as ISO14001, provide specifications for management systems that an organisation can deploy to deal with its environmental impact. There are sometimes financial incentives for certification in different countries and/or states.

There are also industry-sponsored standards, such as the IBM Energy Efficiency Program.

Carbon trading

Carbon trading provides a market-driven, as opposed to a penalty-driven, approach to reducing CO_2 emissions and increasing the use of sustainable energy.

The advantage of legislation and taxation, from a social enforcement perspective, is obviously that potentially it has greater reach, and that it can be enforced. For example, the WEEE Directive enforces the safe disposal of all electrical and electronic products that fall within its remit and jurisdiction.

However, because legislation is often driven by political motives, laws don't always resolve the problem they purport to address. George Spafford, Principal Consultant at Pepperweed Consulting says that 'Government regulation typically requires additional costs'. For example, the Sarbanes-Oxley (SOX) regulation has resulted in greater long-term data storage costs. With regard to regulation on increasing the energy efficiency of data centres, George Spafford says that 'there isn't uniform agreement about how to measure IT's energy utilisation and efficiency'. He then takes this a step further and argues that one of the risks of not increasing the energy efficiency of data centres is the threat of regulation.

Carbon trading, rather than being punitive in intent, is market- and incentive-driven. There are many who argue that incentives are more effective than punitive measures[4] for

---

[4] *A Proposal for Stewardship Support to Private Native Forests in NSW*, The University of Queensland, Vanclay et al, 2006,

bringing about changes in behaviour. The David Suzuki Foundation argues that the difficulty with taxation is to make it 'effective, fair, and properly targeted'.[5] They also quote several studies which have shown that

the single most effective solution to rising greenhouse gas emissions is using the market to put a price on carbon. Putting a price on carbon, through a cap-and-trade system, is a more broadly effective approach than subsidies, voluntary programmes and more effective than regulations in most instances.[6]

The obvious disadvantage of carbon trading is the risk that the profit-driven approach will not always result in an outcome which meets the environmental aims. Clean Air-Cool Planet, a US non-profit environmental organisation, describe the newness of carbon trading (March 2008)[7]:

Environmental commodity markets are still relatively new; the retail market for voluntary carbon neutrality is newer still. One implication of this is that the market is still catching up with public interest. There are no widely accepted standards, for example, as to what qualifies as an 'offset' for purposes of making consumers carbon neutral. As a result, one can still question what consumers are actually buying when they purchase carbon neutrality for themselves, their family, or their vehicle. In the absence of an accepted standard, almost anyone can offer to sell you almost anything and claim that this purchase will make you carbon neutral. Because a carbon offset is an intangible commodity, it is very

---

http://search.arrow.edu.au/main/results?c_subject0=Land+and+Parks+Management+(300902)&c_subject1=Natural+Resource+Management+(300803)&start=0&tc_subject=land.

[5] *Everything you wanted to know about offsetting but were afraid to ask*, April 2007, Zero Footprint.

[6] *Pricing carbon: saving green*, David Suzuki Foundation, 2008.

[7] *A Consumer's Guide to Retail Carbon Offset Providers*, Clean Air-Cool Planet, March 2008, www.cleanair-coolplanet.org/ConsumersGuidetoCarbonOffsets.pdf.

difficult for consumers – even environmentally savvy ones – to differentiate between a high-quality and a low-quality offering.

CHAPTER 1: LEGISLATIVE INITIATIVES

The table below provides an overview of the key global legislative and fiscal environmental initiatives.

Name	Description	Where impl'd
RoHS	Use of hazardous materials in the manufacture of products	EU California China
Top Runner program	Energy efficiency of ICT products	Japan
WEEE	Disposal of electronic products	EU
Electronic Waste Recycling Act (EWRA)	Disposal of electronic products	California
The Promotion of Effective Utilization of Resources	Disposal of electronic products	Japan
The Resource Recycling of Electrical and Electronic Equipment and Vehicles	Disposal of electronic products	South Korea
Lieberman-Warner Climate Security Act	Reduction of CO_2 emissions (currently postponed)	US

Climate Change Levy	Improved energy efficiency and reduction of CO_2 emissions	UK

Table 1: An overview of the key global legislative and fiscal environmental initiatives

The scope of product-related legislation is international, because electronic goods are sold internationally. For example, the Restriction of the Use of Certain Hazardous Substances in Electrical and Electronic Equipment (RoHS) is a European-initiated directive which also affects the specification for the manufacturing of goods in the US. This is because manufacturers in the US who export goods to the EU must comply with the European RoHS.[8] There is also a regulation in California which requires RoHS compliance for goods sold within California.[9]

Envirowise[10] has calculated the costs to the UK economy to comply with these directives. They estimate that these costs are £120 million per year over 10 years for capital and research and development costs to comply with the RoHS Directive; £217–£455 million per year to comply with the WEEE Directive, and £55–£96 million per year for increased operating costs from using alternative substances in order to comply with the RoHS Directive.[11]

---

[8] '"Green" is Hot for Storage Managers Baltimore MD', Marty Foltyn, Internet.com,
http://articles.directorym.net/Green_Is_Hot_for_Storage_Managers_Ba
ltimore_MD-r896094-Baltimore_MD.html.
[9] 'What is RoHS?', California Department of Toxic Substances Control, www.dtsc.ca.gov/HazardousWaste/RoHS.cfm.
[10] See www.envirowise.gov.uk.
[11] *Sustainable design of electrical and electronic products to control costs and comply with legislation*, Envirowise,
www.envirowise.gov.uk/GG427.

The Market Transformation Programme (MTP) says that there is not any currently implemented European legislation which 'addresses ICT energy consumption ... the Top Runner scheme in Japan provides an example of such an approach, and the EuP Directive is likely to contain energy requirements in an implementing agreement for ICT in and around 2009/2010'.[12]

[12] *Sustainable product legislation relevant to ICT*, Market Transformation Programme, 31/3/2008, www.mtprog.com/spm/download/document/id/690.

CHAPTER 2: ROHS

The RoHS Directive will have a far-reaching impact on the manufacture of electronic equipment.

The RoHS, EU Directive 2002/95/EC, was adopted in February 2003 by the European Union.[13] It took effect in the UK[14] on 1 July 2006 and is required to be made law and enforced in each EU member state. This directive restricts (see Table 2, below) the use of six hazardous materials in the manufacture of various types of electronic and electrical equipment.

RoHS applies to companies that manufacture or assemble electrical or electronic equipment within the EU, that import electrical or electronic equipment from outside Europe, or that (again, within Europe) re-badge electronic products as their own. Producers must ensure that products do not contain specified hazardous substances and that they prepare appropriate documentation. Restrictions apply per homogenous material by weight.

---

[13] 'Directive 2002/95/EC of the European Parliament and of the Council of 27 January 2003', http://eur-lex.europa.eu/LexUriServ/LexUriServ.do?uri=OJ:L:2003:037:0019:00 23:EN:PDF.

[14] 'What is RoHS?', www.rohs.gov.uk.

	EU
Restricted substances and maximum concentration value percentage by weight	**Lead – 0.1%** **Cadmium – 0.01%** **Mercury – 0.1%** **Hexavalent chromium – 0.1%** **Polybrominated biphenyls (PBBs) – 0.1%** **Polybrominated diphenyl ethers (PBDEs) – 0.1%**
Scope of products covered under the Act	**Applies to 'electrical and electronic equipment' which fall under WEEE categories one to seven and 10**
Marking	**None**

Table 2: The RoHS requirements

Source: 1. 'What is RoHS', www.rohs.gov.uk

The State of California developed its own version[15] of this law, modelled on RoHS, and the California[16] RoHS Law took effect on 1 January 2007. It is considered unlikely that RoHS-like regulation will be adopted at a federal level in the US in the near to medium term.

---

[15] 'How Do the California Restrictions on the use of Certain Hazardous Substances (RoHS) Law and Regulations Compare to the European Union's RoHS Directive?', California Government, www.dtsc.ca.gov/HazardousWaste/RoHS_CAvEU.cfm.
[16] 'What is RoHS?', California Department of Toxic Substances Control, www.dtsc.ca.gov/HazardousWaste/RoHS.cfm.

In China, the 'Management Methods for Controlling Pollution Caused by Electronic Information Products Regulation' ('China RoHS') was put into effect by China's Ministry of Information Industry (MII) on 28 February 2006.[17] The scope of the China RoHS was developed independently of the EU RoHS. It applies the same percentages as the EU directive, but only to lead, cadmium, mercury and hexavalent chromium

Another law that addresses the sustainability of ICT products is the Japanese Top Runner Program. The aim of this programme is to improve energy efficiency. The programme includes ICT product groups, and focuses on energy performance. Manufacturers need to ensure that the energy efficiency of their products meets the standard. Further information can be found on the Japanese site:

www.eccj.or.jp/top_runner/index.html.

---

[17] 'China Finalizes "RoHS" Regulation: Overview of Requirements', AeA,
www.aeanet.org/GovernmentAffairs/gabl_ChinaRoHSpage0905.asp.

CHAPTER 3: ELECTRICAL WASTE DISPOSAL

Organisations have long been subject to the Duty of Care regulations[18] (part of the 1990 Environmental Protection Act), which oblige them to ensure that business waste, including electronic waste, is disposed of in a responsible manner. This obligation includes ensuring that any waste contractor is correctly licensed as they could be held responsible for any of their waste which is fly-tipped. Of course, there may also be security (confidentiality of information and Data Protection Act) considerations relating to waste disposal that may need to be considered.

Hazardous Waste Regulations[19] are also likely to apply to some electrical equipment including, for instance, cathode ray tubes, fluorescent tubes and lead-acid batteries. Organisations should already have appropriate processes in place for dealing with waste (which will originate from across the organisation, rather than just in IT) that falls within the ambit of these regulations.

There are two sets of regulation that are specifically relevant to the IT organisation in the EU. The first is the WEEE regulations, and the second is the EU Batteries Directive.

EU WEEE Directive

Legislation for the disposal of electronic equipment is covered within Europe by the Waste Electrical and Electronic Equipment (WEEE) Directive. The WEEE Directive aims to 'encourage the design and production of electrical and electronic equipment to facilitate its repair, possible upgrading, re-use, disassembly and recycling at end of life'.[20]

---

[18] Here's a good summary description of these regulations: *www.brookes.ac.uk/eie/doc.htm*.

[19] *www.environment-agency.gov.uk/business/topics/waste/32180.aspx*.

[20] *Sustainable product legislation relevant to ICT*, Market Transformation Programme, 31/3/2008, *www.mtprog.com/spm/download/document/id/690*.

The UK Regulations implementing the WEEE Directive became active on 1 July 2007. The regulations were later amended to clarify how reuse can be counted as part evidence of compliance and the recording of WEEE arising.

The WEEE Regulations apply to the producers, retailers and distributors, local authorities, exporters and re-processors, and businesses and other non-household users of EEE.[21] New products are required to be marked with the WEEE symbol, to indicate that they must not be disposed of in a municipal waste collection facility.

Within ICT, WEEE applies to IT and telecommunications equipment, and also accessories such as keyboards and connecting cables.

Figure 1: The WEEE logo

Source: The European Communities

This legislation compels manufacturers of equipment to take responsibility for their waste, either themselves or through a government-approved waste-handling firm. This is known as extended producer responsibility (EPR). Peeters says that:

---

[21] *Sustainable product legislation relevant to ICT*, Market Transformation Programme, 31/3/2008, *www.mtprog.com/spm/download/document/id/690*.

A producer must provide information in the form of manuals on reuse and environmentally sound treatment for each new type of product they put on the market.

The information should identify the different components and materials and the location of any dangerous substances in the hardware.

Retailers have the option to offer in-store take back, or to join the collective take-back scheme run by Valpak. In joining Valpak, all WEEE will be sent to the nearest civil amenity sites that have been upgraded to a designated collection facility.'[22]

The EU are obliged to review the WEEE Directive of 2002 five years after the EU implementation. The EU has consulted on proposals to revise the WEEE Directive.[23] The EU are currently revising the WEEE Directive and it is expected that the EU will soon publish proposals to amend the WEEE Directive.

Here, in simple format as laid down on the BERR website[24], are the current WEEE responsibilities:

- If you bought electrical equipment before 13 August 2005, and are replacing it with new equipment fulfilling the same function, then **the producer of the new equipment** is responsible for the collection, treatment and recycling of the old equipment, regardless of whether they were the original manufacturer.
- If you bought the equipment before 13 August 2005 and do not replace it, then **you** are responsible for financing and arranging treatment in accordance with the WEEE

---

[22] 'Waste not, want not', Michael Peeters and Helen Keele, *Computing*, 24 July 2008,
www.computing.co.uk/computing/analysis/2222191/waste-4127840?page=2.

[23] 'Waste not, want not', Michael Peeters and Helen Keele, *Green Computing*, 24 July 2008,
www.whatpc.co.uk/computing/analysis/2222191/waste-4127840.

[24] WEEE – Business User Factsheet from BERR.

Regulations and existing waste management legislation, including the Duty of Care and the Hazardous Waste Regulations.

- If you bought electrical equipment after 13 August 2005, then the **producer of that equipment** is responsible for its collection, treatment and recycling when you dispose of it.
- If you lease or rent equipment, the producer is usually responsible for its disposal.

Businesses must therefore be prepared to arrange and pay for the transfer of WEEE to an approved Authorised Treatment Facility if

a) it was acquired before 13 August 2005, and is not being replaced with equivalent EEE;
b) the producer (or its compliance scheme) cannot be traced; or
c) a business is buying new EEE and, as part of the negotiated price, accepts the future cost of treatment and disposal.

Critics of the WEEE Directive claim that many importers of equipment from outside Europe are unaware of WEEE obligations. A recent survey carried out by the manufacturer Dell and the Federation for Small Businesses (FSB) found that 22.5% of respondents did not know whether or not WEEE applied to their businesses.[25]

EU Batteries Directive

The EU Batteries Directive 2006[26] banned the sale from 1991 of batteries and accumulators containing more than 0.0005% of mercury by weight, introduced an EU-wide registration procedure for battery producers and a framework for collection

---

[25] 'Dell/FSB Research Reveals One In Five Small And Medium Enterprises (SMEs) Unaware Of Who The WEEE Directive Applies To', Dell, *www1.euro.dell.com/content/topics/topic.aspx/emea/corporate/pressoff ice/2008/uk/en/2008_06_25_brk_001?c=uk&l=en&s=corp.*
[26] This extended the earlier 1991 directive.

and recycling of batteries. These regulations are still subject to consultation[27] but, in the interim, IT organisations should take appropriate steps to ensure that batteries are separately disposed of.

EU Packaging and Packaging Waste Directive

All IT organisations have to deal with packaging; virtually every new item purchased, from a manual to a piece of computer equipment, will come with packaging. The EU directive[28] requires producers of packaging waste (who meet two threshold tests in terms of their size) to recover and recycle specific tonnages of packaging waste each year. These obligations do not, however, apply to end-users. However, the Green IT organisation will nevertheless take steps to:

- minimise the amount of packaging it receives, for instance by negotiating with suppliers to deliver goods unpackaged or with reduced packaging, and ensure that this is reflected in reduced pricing
- require suppliers to collect and recycle their packaging, in line with their obligations under the Directive, with a consequent reduction in your own waste disposal costs
- ensure that packaging is recycled efficiently and through a licensed waste disposal organisation
- ensure that waste packaging is separated (e.g. cardboard separated from plastic) and not mixed with other (or hazardous) items, in order to maximise the likelihood of it being recycled and to ensure that you are able to benefit from the keenest waste disposal prices from your contractors. Doing this effectively will depend on the provision of appropriate, correctly labelled disposal containers and an ongoing programme of staff awareness and training.

---

[27] *www.berr.gov.uk/whatwedo/sectors/sustainability/ batteries/page49501.html.*
[28] *www.defra.gov.uk/environment/waste/topics/ packaging/regulations.htm.*

Other waste legislation

Within the US there is no federal law that covers the disposal of electronic equipment. Different states have adopted different rules and regulations, which creates a challenge for manufacturers.[29] The Computer TakeBack Campaign provides advice on the disposal of electronic waste within the US. California has passed SB 20: Electronic Waste Recycling Act of 2003, or EWRA. Other US states and cities are debating whether to adopt similar laws, and there are several states that have mercury and PBDE bans already.

The Japanese Law for the Promotion of Effective Utilization of Resources came into effect in April 2001. The aim of the law is to promote the reuse and recycling of products.[30] In South Korea, the Korean Act for the Resource Recycling of Electrical and Electronic Equipment and Vehicles came into effect in April 2007.[31]

---

[29] 'The Promise and Pitfalls of E-Waste Takeback', Greener Computing, *www.greenercomputing.com/feature/2008/05/14/the-promise-and-pitfalls-e-waste-takeback*.
[30] *Law for the Promotion of Effective Utilization of Resources*, *www.meti.go.jp/policy/recycle/main/english/law/promotion.html*.
[31] 'Korea RoHS/WEEE/ELV', *www.designchainassociates.com/korearohs.html*.

CHAPTER 4: CLIMATE CHANGE LAWS

While carbon trading and cap-and-trade initiatives are a key component of society-wide efforts to reduce greenhouse gas emissions (these schemes are discussed in greater detail in Chapter 7), there are still only a small number of statutory schemes.

The RGGI cap-and-trade initiative

The Regional Greenhouse Gas Initiative (RGGI) is the first mandatory cap-and-trade programme in the US for CO_2 emissions. It is a collaborative initiative between 10 US states: Connecticut, Delaware, Maine, Massachusetts, Maryland, New Hampshire, New Jersey, New York, Rhode Island and Vermont. RGGI was effective from 1 January 2009 and is aimed at reducing the CO_2 emitted by power plants. It is anticipated that there will be a small increase in electricity charges passed on to consumers. It is also anticipated that RGGI will be used as a model for a federal cap-and-trade scheme, and for the EU's ETS.[32]

However, critics of RGGI have suggested that the prices for carbon permits are so low that the initiative is unlikely to make much difference at least in the short term.[33]

Western Climate Initiative (WCI)

The WCI is a mandatory cap-and-trade initiative aimed at reducing CO_2 emissions by the western states of the US and Canada. The participating states are California, Arizona, Montana, New Mexico, Oregon, Utah, Washington, Ontario,

---

[32] Regional Greenhouse Gas Initiative, RGGI, *www.rggi.org/docs/RGGI_Executive_Summary.pdf*.
[33] RGGI's Rules: Northeast Launches First U.S. Carbon Cap, But Will It Work? Keith Johnson, 25 Sept 2008, *http://blogs.wsj.com/environmentalcapital/2008/09/25/rggis-rules-northeast-launches-first-us-carbon-cap-but-will-it-work*.

Quebec, British Columbia and Manitoba. The aim is to reduce greenhouse gas emissions by 15% below 2005 levels by 2020.

UK Climate Change Levy

The UK's Climate Change Levy (CCL) is a 'tax on the use of energy with offsetting cuts in employers' National Insurance contributions and additional support for energy efficiency schemes and renewable sources of energy'.[34] The aim of the levy is to encourage users to improve energy efficiency and to reduce emissions of greenhouse gases. The levy was introduced in the budget of 1999, and came into operation in 2001.

The levy is applicable to all businesses with the exception of[35] small businesses that use a domestic amount of energy. The levy is also not applicable to organisations in the transport sector, with the exception of those organisations using energy to run transport at theme parks or historical transport such as trams in museums.

Businesses pay the levy through their fuel bills. The tax is offset by reductions in National Insurance contributions.

Businesses which are 'energy intensive' may be able to get an 80% discount on the CCL by taking out a climate change agreement with their respective trade association. However, this does mean that the organisation has to meet specific targets for improving energy efficiency or reducing CO_2 emissions.

CCL applies to all fuels with the exception of:

- oil-based fuels (which are already subject to excise duty)
- fuels used to produce other forms of energy, for example, in electricity generation

---

[34] 'Climate change agreements', Department for Environment Food and Rural Affairs,
www.defra.gov.uk/environment/climatechange/uk/business/cca/index.htm.
[35] 'Climate change levy (CCL)', NetRegs, 21 August 2008,
www.netregs.gov.uk/netregs/62973.aspx.

- natural gas in Northern Ireland (until 31 March 2011)
- combined heat and power systems meeting the DEFRA quality assurance programme
- energy from renewable sources, except large hydroelectric schemes and some energy from waste facilities
- energy supplies not used as fuel, such as feedstock for electrolytic processes and aluminium smelting
- fuel used as a raw material, for example coal used to make carbon filters.

The current CCL rates since April 2008 are:

Fuel type	Charge
Electricity	0.456p/kWh (pence per kilowatt hour)
Gas	0.159p/kWh
Coal	1.242p/kg (pence per kilogram)
Liquid petroleum gas (LPG)	1.018p/kg

Table 3: The current CCL rates since April 2008

Organisations paying the CCL also receive a reduction in National Insurance. This means that, depending on the amount of energy used, some organisations incur a net gain, whereby the reduction in National Insurance contributions is greater than the amount paid in tax. Conversely, some organisations incur a net loss. The Confederation of British Industry (CBI), in conjunction with the Engineering Employers' Federation (EEF) undertook a survey on the impact of the CCL on businesses. They found that the impact of the CCL varied between sectors.[36] The manufacturing sector was hardest hit, with a £328 million ($604 million) rise in energy bills and a £185 million ($340 million) cut in National Insurance contributions,[37] resulting in a net loss of £143 million ($263 million).

The mining and utilities sectors were also negatively affected. The majority of the services sector achieved a net gain.

Criticisms of the CCL have argued that this isn't an equitable means of increasing energy efficiency or of reducing CO_2 emissions. The CBI[38] says that the CCL is 'an imperfect proxy for a carbon tax with electricity from nuclear and coal generation being levied at the same rate'. The CBI have called for the CCL to be reformed 'so that it better reflects the carbon content of the energy source provided (i.e. zero rating electricity generated from nuclear sources and reflecting the carbon content of gas vs. coal generated electricity)'.[39] The CBI also criticised the CCL, which it says 'damaged the competitiveness of more than half the UK's manufacturers'.[40]

---

[36] *CBI response to the environmental audit committee inquiry on the role of the climate change levy and agreements*, CBI, October 2007, www.cbi.org.uk/ndbs/positiondoc.nsf/1f08ec61711f29768025672a0055 f7a8/8BA78681D515B14880257380005A7482/$file/envirocclresp0110 07.pdf.

[37] '"Flawed" energy tax is damaging manufacturers while failing to deliver on energy efficiency', CBI News release, 31 October 2002, www.cbi.org.uk/ndbs/press.nsf/0363c1f07c6ca12a8025671c00381cc7/ 54299262a055d64880256c5200347524?OpenDocument.

[38] 'CBI response to the environmental audit committee inquiry on the role of the climate change levy and agreements', CBI, October 2007, www.cbi.org.uk/ndbs/positiondoc.nsf/1f08ec61711f29768025672a0055 f7a8/8BA78681D515B14880257380005A7482/$file/envirocclresp0110 07.pdf.

[39] 'CBI response to the environmental audit committee inquiry on the role of the climate change levy and agreements', CBI, October 2007, www.cbi.org.uk/ndbs/positiondoc.nsf/1f08ec61711f29768025672a0055 f7a8/8BA78681D515B14880257380005A7482/$file/envirocclresp0110 07.pdf.

[40] 'Flawed energy tax is damaging manufacturers while failing to deliver on energy efficiency', CBI News release, 31 October 2002,

4: Climate Change Laws

The UK Government commissioned Cambridge Econometrics to evaluate the impact of the levy. The consequent report, which was published in 2005, found that total CO_2 emissions were reduced by 3.1mtC (million tonnes of carbon) (2.0%) in 2002. Similarly, there was a decline in the use of gas and electricity use by 4.8% and 3.6% respectively.

www.cbi.org.uk/ndbs/press.nsf/0363c1f07c6ca12a8025671c00381cc7/
54299262a055d64880256c5200347524?OpenDocument.

CHAPTER 5: FISCAL INITIATIVES AND STANDARDS

The following table provides an overview of the key global environmental standards, advisory services and government-backed financial incentives.

Name	Description	Where implemented
ENERGY STAR	Energy efficiency labelling of product	US, EU, Australia, Canada, Japan, New Zealand, Taiwan
Climate Savers Computing Initiative	This organisation works in conjunction with ENERGY STAR. It provides a product catalogue of energy-saving IT equipment.	US
80 PLUS program	Initiated by the US Government, this is a forum between government and industry providing free advice and certification for power supply	US

	products with high efficiency performance.	
'Computers Off Australia'	Private organisation that 'promotes sensible power management and reduces the carbon footprint'. It provides lists of energy-efficient IT equipment.	Australia
EuP	Environmental impact of product	EU
IBM Energy Efficiency Program	Reduction of electricity in data centres	US, Europe
Energy Efficiency Loan scheme	Incentive to purchase energy-efficient product	UK
Enhanced capital allowances	Incentive to purchase energy-efficient product	UK

Table 4: An overview of the key global environmental standards, advisory services and government-induced financial incentives

ENERGY STAR

ENERGY STAR is an international standard which is used to measure energy-efficient ratings. Products bearing the 'ENERGY STAR' label are deemed to be more energy-efficient than those that don't meet the grade, according to the ENERGY STAR specifications.

The ENERGY STAR programme was created in 1992 by the US EPA. Agreements to promote ENERGY STAR-qualified products have been made with the European Union,[41] Australia, Canada, Japan, New Zealand and Taiwan.[42]

Devices carrying the ENERGY STAR logo, such as computer products and peripherals, kitchen appliances, buildings and other products, save 20–30% electricity on average.[43] ENERGY STAR-qualified office and imaging products use 30–75% less electricity than 'standard' equipment.

ENERGY STAR predicts that the energy savings resulting from using ENERGY STAR products will save nearly $5 billion a year.[44][45]

---

[41] 'Commissioner Piebalgs welcomes adoption of the new Energy Star programme', EUROPA,
http://europa.eu/rapid/pressReleasesAction.do?reference=IP/07/1943 &format=HTML&aged=0&language=EN&guiLanguage=en.

[42] 'Who's Working With ENERGY STAR? International Partners', ENERGY STAR,
www.energystar.gov/index.cfm?c=partners.intl_implementation.

[43] 'If your appliances are avocado, they probably aren't green', Alina Tugend, 10 May 2008,
www.nytimes.com/2008/05/10/business/yourmoney/10shortcuts.html?s cp=1&sq=appliances%20avocado%20green&st=cse.

[44] 'New Specifications for Many Office Products in 2007', ENERGY STAR,
www.energystar.gov/index.cfm?c=ofc_equip.pr_office_equipment.

**Figure 2: Products meeting this standard display a label
with the ENERGY STAR logo.**

In 2007, new ENERGY STAR specifications for office
equipment were brought out.[46] These specifications cover
desktop computers, integrated computer systems, notebook
computers, tablet PCs, desktop-derived servers and
workstations.

ENERGY STAR is currently developing a product
specification for enterprise servers. This will include computer
servers with up to four processor sockets, blade servers and
storage, DC servers, storage equipment, network equipment
and power supplies. UPS are not covered under the scope of
this specification. It was anticipated that the new product list
would be available in January 2009.[47] The new specifications
provide energy savings and also set additional energy saving
requirements for accessories, such as an external power adapter
or cordless handset.

---

[45] *Building a Powerful and Enduring Brand: The Past, Present, and
Future of the ENERGY STAR® Brand*, Prepared by Interbrand for the
US Environmental Protection Agency June 2007,
*www.energystar.gov/ia/partners/downloads/ENERGY_STARBndManf5
08.pdf.*
[46] 'New Specifications for Many Office Products in 2007', ENERGY
STAR,
www.energystar.gov/index.cfm?c=ofc_equip.pr_office_equipment.
[47] *Putting the Green into IT*, IBM, 2008.

ENERGY STAR also provides recommendations for the power management of monitors and computers, so that they consume less electricity when not being used and go into 'sleep' mode.[48] There are also commercial and open source products available which enable sleep features to be activated across networks of computers. ENERGY STAR provides advice on selecting the most appropriate product.

In addition, the EPA is also working on a data centre rating system for a possible ENERGY STAR programme for data centres. The metric is likely to be largely based on infrastructure efficiency, including energy losses through power conversion and the UPS. Linked US Government-based initiatives also include:

- DOE Save Energy Now and ENERGY STAR are developing tools to assist data centre operators in characterising their energy use and identifying opportunities for improvement. These include the DC Pro tool suite and the EPA ENERGY STAR Portfolio Manager tool.
- A certification programme for data centre energy efficiency experts, developed by the DOE.
- A recognition of those data centres which have demonstrated a defined level of energy savings. ENERGY STAR will provide the ENERGY STAR label for those data centres that achieve a high level of energy performance.
- The DOE and Federal Energy Management Program (FEMP) are developing guidelines for the specification and design of newly constructed Federal data centres.

The Fact Sheet on National Data Center Energy Efficiency Information Program, (from the US Department of Energy (DOE) and US Environmental Protection Agency (EPA), 19 March 2008) provides additional information and a list of resources.

---

[48] 'General Technical Overview of Power Management', ENERGY STAR, *www.energystar.gov/index.cfm?c=power_mgt.pr_power_management*.

EuP

An important component of the international legal framework is the EU Directive on the Eco-Design of Energy-Using Products 2005/32/EC (the EuP Directive).[49]

The aim of this Directive is to reduce the environmental impact of products throughout their life cycle.[50] The UK Department for Environment, Food and Rural Affairs (DEFRA) describes this as including environmental impacts resulting from[51] 'product manufacture (processes and materials used), usage (energy/water consumption and emissions) and disposal (waste generation)'.

In the same way that consumers may look at miles per gallon before purchasing a car, EuP provides information about the 'energy' rating of a product. However, the difference is that the energy rating, as well as covering energy use, also considers the environmental impact that the product will make throughout its entire life cycle.

The EuP Directive provides for setting of eco-design requirements which EuPs must meet before they can be placed on the market. Suppliers will be required to provide data on parts and subassemblies to manufacturers.

Manufacturers will need to provide information to consumers on the role consumers can play in reducing the product impact and information on environmental characteristics to assist consumers in making choices. The focus of EuP is on volume and large energy-using products. The number of products within the scope of EuP is very large, and it applies to products using any form of energy during their use.

---

[49] 'Eco-Design of Energy-Using Products',
http://ec.europa.eu/enterprise/eco_design/index_en.htm.
[50] 'EcoDesign (EuP) Directive Compliance Services', ERA Technology, *www.era.co.uk/Services/ecodesign.asp*.
[51] *Guidance notes on the Eco-design for Energy-using Products Regulations*, DEFRA, August 2007,
www.defra.gov.uk/environment/consumerprod/pdf/energy-products-regs-guide.pdf.

Figure 3: The EuP label

Source: European Commission, Eco-design of energy-using products
http://ec.europa.eu/avservices/photo/photo_search_en.cfm?key
word=energy+efficiency&videoref © European Communities,
1995–2009

The EuP Directive has been implemented in the UK by means of The Eco-Design for Energy Using Products Regulations 2007. This came into force on 11 August 2007 and currently covers boilers, fridges/freezers and ballasts for fluorescent lights.

The enforcement bodies are the local trading standards[52] agencies. These regulations make it an offence to sell products that do not meet the EuP energy efficiency standards, and there is a maximum fine for non-compliance of £5,000.

The European Commission has published a draft plan listing the next range of products to be considered under the EuP Directive, including IT servers and data storage equipment. The plan sets out a list of product groups that will be considered as priorities for the three years following July 2007.

---

[52] 'Energy Using Products Directive', Mark Shayler, ECO[3],
www.iema.net/download/events/midlands/9%20April%20EuP.ppt.

The EC is also considering a measure relating to standby and off-mode of household and office equipment.[53] The draft plan is currently out for review. If accepted it will be published at the beginning of 2009 and come into force at the beginning of 2010.[54]

The Market Transformation Programme (MTP) supports the development and implementation of UK Government policy on sustainable products. The Market Transformation Programme is a series of 12 consultation papers which set out how performance of energy-using products will need to improve between now and 2020, including proposals for product standards and targets to phase out the least efficient products. The result of this consultation process will be a set of 'product standards which will be reviewed annually and which will be used to guide and support government policy relating to EU standards and labelling as well as to encourage UK retailers, manufacturers and service providers to bring forward more energy-efficient products'.[55]

The MTP have also produced a 'What-If?' tool which presents a range of scenarios on the future energy consumption until 2020 for nearly 30 domestic and commercial products.[56] The tool enables manufacturers and consumers to:

- 'evaluate existing product performance data'
- 'evaluate future impacts on resources from use of the product'
- 'study product use impact on the environment'.

---

[53] 'EU Committee Agrees Implementing Measure Establishing Standards for Stand-by and Off Mode Losses', Market Transformation Programme, 14 July 2008, _www.mtprog.com/cms/eu-committee-agrees-implementing-measure-establishing-standards-for-stand-by-and-off-mode-losses_.

[54] 'Study for preparing the first Working Plan of the EcoDesign Directive', EPTA, _www.epta.gr/xar/index.php/eco_.

[55] _Consultation on sustainable products – improving the efficiency of energy using products_, Market Transformation Programme, _www.mtprog.com/spm/download/document/id/690_.

[56] 'Let's discover What-If', _http://whatif.mtprog.com_.

CHAPTER 6: ENVIRONMENTAL MANAGEMENT STANDARDS

ISO14001

Environmental management is a challenge for many organisations and an international standard for effective environmental management has emerged over the last 15 years. Modelled on aspects of ISO9001 (which has now been taken up by nearly one million organisations worldwide), ISO14001 is the best practice standard for the systematic management of an organisation's environmental impacts.

ISO14001 is the international specification for an environmental management system (EMS). It is broken down into five sections[57]:

1. General requirements
2. Environmental policy
3. Planning implementation and operation
4. Checking and corrective action
5. Management review

It is relevant to all organisations, in all sectors, and of all sizes. It is not product-specific and is vendor-agnostic.

ISO14001 requires organisations to publish a policy statement that describes the organisation's environmental values, and then to ensure that its actual performance is consistent with this statement. This requires an environmental risk assessment, operational control and the setting of specific, measurable, achievable, realistic and timebound (SMART) objectives to achieve its strategic environmental goals.

The standard has set requirements that should be followed in order for an organisation to be compliant, but these can be

---

[57] 'ISO14001 Environment', BSi, _www.bsi-global.com/en/Assessment-and-certification-services/management-systems/Standards-and-Schemes/ISO-14001_.

modified to suit the business activity. ISO14001 recommends that organisations should set realistic targets. The standard concentrates on companys' working processes and activities, rather than measurements such as the number of lights switched off, quantity of paper used, and so on.

The environmental objectives are achieved through the implementation of management programmes.

BSi positions environmental management squarely within an organisation's CSR activity and claims that ISO14001 enables organisations to:

- demonstrate a commitment to achieving legal and regulatory compliance to regulators and to government
- demonstrate their environmental commitment to stakeholders
- demonstrate an innovative and forward-thinking approach to customers and prospective employees
- increase their access to new customers and business partners
- better manage their environmental risks, now and in the future
- potentially reduce public liability insurance costs
- reduce operational costs through reduced energy consumption and use of natural resources
- reduce fines and clean-up costs
- enhance their reputation.

EMAS

Some regulators and policy makers prefer the EU's Eco-Management and Audit Scheme (EMAS) to ISO14001, as they believe it offers them more transparency, credibility and reliability.[58] The Institute of Environmental Management & Assessment (IEMA), who are the 'competent body' for EMAS, claim that the scheme is completely compatible with ISO14001, but goes further in its requirements for performance

---

[58] 'Corporate Social Responsibility', A Government update.

improvement, employee involvement, legal compliance and communication with stakeholders.[59]

The IEMA reports that EMAS enables organisations to:

- make more sustainable use of resources
- demonstrate responsible management of environmental risks
- improve relations with environmental regulators
- comply with regulations, environmental laws, and voluntary or contractual agreements
- maximise business opportunities in the market place
- show evidence of good management to investors and insurers
- respond to growing expectations and pressures for environmental reporting
- communicate more effectively with stakeholders
- modernise their management
- enhance the quality of products and services
- make validated green claims about products, services and activities
- enrich the process of environmental innovation and hasten the move to more sustainable means of production and consumption
- motivate staff and involve employees in delivering the environmental management system
- improve individual and public health.

Our view is that, when considering whether to pursue ISO14001 or EMAS, ISO14001 has the advantage and benefit of being an international accredited certification scheme. ISO14001 also has many elements in common with ISO9001 and other well-established management systems and, therefore, perhaps a greater degree of recognition amongst those who feel encouraged to start the development of an EMS.

---

[59] EMAS, *www.emas.org.uk/aboutemas/mainframe.htm*.

ISO27001

Disposal of computer equipment raises the issue of how data that is on that equipment – usually stored on a hard drive, for instance – is to be dealt with.

ISO/IEC 27001 is the international standard for information security management and, while it has no direct role in environmental management, it does at least address the issue of the secure disposal of information assets. Control A.9.2.6. of ISO/IEC 27001 requires that information and licensed software is erased from all equipment prior to its disposal or reuse.[60]

Data protection obligations (which take different forms around the world) all extend to data at any stage in its life cycle, and organisations disposing of computer equipment that contains personally identifiable data (PID) will usually have a legal obligation to ensure that all PID is deleted from computer equipment prior to disposal, and that this PID cannot in any way be recovered.

The 'delete' function in software packages is not sufficient; equipment to be disposed of needs to be completely and securely wiped of all data. Due to the relatively low cost of disk drives, it may be better to destroy disk drives completely before selling PCs, rather than relying on third parties to wipe them. Storage devices such as floppy disks, CD-ROMs and memory sticks should also be destroyed rather than reused. Workstations, servers and laptops should at the least have their hard disks overwritten prior to their disposal and all software removed. Organisations offering to destroy hard drives prior to disposing of PCs should be able to provide clear evidence that they do this.

---

[60] *IT Governance: A Manager's Guide to Data Security and ISO27001/ISO27002*, 4th edition, Alan Calder and Steve Watkins, 2008.

IBM Energy Efficiency Program

IBM has announced[61] a corporate-led initiative to enable clients to earn energy efficiency certificates for reducing the energy used to run their data centres. Customers who successfully demonstrate energy reduction and efficiency can earn energy efficiency certificates from Neuwing Energy Ventures[62]. These certificates can then be traded on the energy efficiency market or used to demonstrate reductions in energy use and reduced CO_2 emissions. The programme has been launched in conjunction with Neuwing Energy. The evaluation used for certification will include looking at virtualisation and resolving data centre design flaws. The programme is currently available in the US with plans to introduce this in Europe at a later date.

The Energy-Efficiency Loans scheme (UK)

The Carbon Trust administers a scheme to provide small and medium-sized UK businesses with interest-free loans of between £5,000 and £10,000, repayable over a period of up to four years, to replace or upgrade existing equipment with a more energy-efficient version. Further details are available from the Carbon Trust website[63].

Enhanced Capital Allowances (UK)

From 2008, businesses can claim 100% tax allowances on capital expenditure on specific products, thereby shortening the investment payback period. The Enhanced Capital Allowance[64] applies to the purchase of:

- energy-saving plant and machinery

---

[61] 'IBM Launches World's First Corporate-Led Energy Efficiency Certificate Program', IBM, 2 November 2007, *www-03.ibm.com/press/us/en/pressrelease/22513.wss*.

[62] *http://neuwingenergy.com/index.php*.

[63] *www.carbontrust.co.uk/energy/takingaction/loans.htm*.

[64] See *www.eca.gov.uk*.

- low carbon dioxide emission cars and natural gas and hydrogen refuelling infrastructure
- water conservation plant and machinery.

CHAPTER 7: CARBON AND CARBON TRADING

Carbon trading is a somewhat nebulous concept because it refers to the potential for trading an absence of CO_2 emissions. It is also a very new concept and the voluntary carbon trading market is largely unregulated. In addition, although the situation has improved over the last year, there is a dearth of comprehensive information on carbon trading.

Carbon trading refers to the trading of 'carbon credits', or reductions in CO_2 emissions. One carbon credit is the equivalent of the reduction of one tonne of CO_2 emissions. A carbon credit is a metric which is used to measure the value of, for instance, carbon offset projects, which are discussed later in this chapter.

The Green Guide defines carbon trading as

The trading of personal, corporate or national credits to maintain and gradually reduce carbon emissions. Companies, nations or individuals who beat the targets can sell the balance as credits to those that exceed their limits. The financial gain should lead to the reduction in emissions over time.[65]

The environmental aim of carbon trading is to combat climate change by improving energy efficiency, reducing CO_2 emissions and/or increasing the amount of sustainable energy which is generated.

Any organisation seeking to reduce its CO_2 emissions needs first to understand its baseline level of CO_2 emissions, and to measure its carbon footprint.

Carbon footprint

The carbon footprint is a measurement of all the greenhouse gases produced by individuals and/or groups. It relates to the

---

[65] 'Carbon Trading', Green Guide, _www.greenguide.co.uk/pgg_simple_.

amount of greenhouse gases produced daily and yearly through burning fossil fuels for electricity, heating and transportation etc. So, for example, driving an average sized car about 12,000 miles a year will generate 3.5 tonnes of CO_2 in that year.

The carbon footprint is measured in units of tonnes (or kg) of carbon dioxide equivalent.[66]

A carbon footprint is made up of a primary and secondary footprint. The primary footprint is a measure of emissions of CO_2 from the burning of fossil fuels in energy consumption and transportation. The secondary footprint is a measure of CO_2 emissions from the life cycle of products and equipment which we use.

The following table shows the main producers of CO_2 by region in 2005:

Region	CO_2 emissions (million tonnes of CO_2)
US & Canada	6,366
China	5,101
EU	3,922
Russia	1,544
Japan	1,214
India	1,147

---

[66] 'What Is A Carbon Footprint?' *www.carbonfootprint.com/carbonfootprint.html*.

Table 5: The main producers of CO$_2$ by region in 2005

Source: Derived from International Energy Agency: Key World Statistics 2007, www.iea.org/Textbase/stats/index.asp, www.iea.org/textbase/nppdf/free/2008/key_stats_2008.pdf

There is developing sense amongst companies that they will have to disclose their carbon emissions. James Murray, editor of BusinessGreen.com says 'over the next few years carbon dioxide is set to emerge as perhaps the strangest form of currency since cavemen first started trading bits of bone'.[67]

IBM, SAS and Lawson provide software tools which enable businesses to report on their company's carbon emissions. Murray says that firms which comply on carbon emissions sooner rather than later are likely to save more money in the long term.

Carbon offset projects

Subscribing to carbon offset projects is an alternative to reducing internal CO$_2$ emissions. Carbon offsetting is how one compensates for CO$_2$ emissions which one has made/is making by funding an equivalent carbon dioxide saving somewhere else.

The range of carbon offset reduction projects is broad. Examples include:

- Renewable energy projects. For example, Carbon Footprint Ltd[68] is working with a project to develop wind energy in India. The aim is to create sustainable energy, thereby reducing CO$_2$ emissions, as well as developing the local economy in India.
- Reforestation. Carbon Footprint Ltd is also working with a reforestation project in Kenya to plant trees. The aims are

[67] 'How to cultivate a green IT policy', *Computing*, 11 September 2008.
[68] 'Clean Energy – Carbon Offset', Carbon Footprint, *www.carbonfootprint.com/offsetalternativeenergy.html*.

to offset CO_2 emissions, but also to 'reduce poverty, provide wildlife habitats and create a brighter future for project team members including orphans and people living with HIV/AIDS'.

- Paper manufacture efficiency upgrade. The Climate Trust[69] is working with a project to reduce the energy used to recycle paper in Canada. The improved efficiency will come from various measures including the removal of production bottlenecks and retrofit of equipment. The benefits to the company will include increasing its paper-recycling capacity and increasing the company's global competitiveness.

- Internet-based carpool matching. The Carbon Trust has worked on a project to reduce CO_2 emissions by increasing the numbers of commuters in Portland who share cars. The system used Internet-based software which matched drivers and location. The project is now complete.

In theory, the buying and selling of carbon offsets provides benefits for the buyer and the seller:

- The seller benefits from the funding for their project.
- The buyer benefits because they can mitigate their own CO_2 emissions by contributing towards 'non-polluting' or sustainable energy.
- It may also be cheaper for a buyer to purchase carbon offsets than to eliminate their own emissions.

The current voluntary offset market is mainly unregulated.[70] There are, as described below, various criteria which should to be considered when purchasing carbon offsets:

---

[69] 'Paper Manufacturer Efficiency Upgrade', The Climate Trust, *www.climatetrust.org/offset_paper.php*.

[70] 'What is a carbon offset?' David Suzuki Foundation, *www.davidsuzuki.org/Climate_Change/What_You_Can_Do/carbon_off sets.asp*.

Additionality

Additionality proves that a carbon offset project makes a difference. A carbon offset provides 'additionality' when that purchase has enabled a project to happen which would not have happened otherwise, by overcoming financial or other barriers to the project. The project is considered additional if it isn't 'business as usual'.

Additionality proves that the purchase of the offset provides a 'net benefit for the climate'.[71]

Project type

Some projects are more viable than others. For example, wind farms are considered viable projects because they directly create sustainable energy.

However, the planting of trees is considered less viable because this does not contribute to creating sustainable energy. There is also concern that 'soil carbon can be disturbed and released by harvesting and reforestation activities'.[72] Other concerns are that a forest is not permanent, they are a source of carbon emissions and also provide a very space-consuming method of reducing CO_2 emissions.

Projects which reduce the amount of ozone-depleting halocarbon gases have also been criticised. This is because the very low cost of this offset has made their purchase very popular, which in turn has made the purchase of offsets which generate sustainable energy less popular. In addition, and in line with the law of unintended consequences, the high profit has actually resulted in more halocarbon gases being created. This is obviously contrary to the overall purpose of carbon offsets.

---

[71] 'What is a carbon offset?' David Suzuki Foundation, *www.davidsuzuki.org/Climate_Change/What_You_Can_Do/carbon_off sets.asp*.
[72] 'The Problems with Carbon Offsets from Tree Planting', David Suzuki Foundation, *www.davidsuzuki.org/Climate_Change/What_You_Can_Do/trees3.asp*.

Unique

The carbon offset should only be sold once. Once the offset is used, it needs to be retired to ensure that the benefit of the reductions is only counted once. A failure to do this is called 'double counting'.

Carbon offset leakage

This happens when a reduction in CO_2 emissions actually causes an increase in CO_2 emissions elsewhere.

Permanency

The project needs to be a permanent one.

Verification

Depending on the scheme, projects need to be verified by a third party auditor, or self-verified. Independent verification has the better track record.

Location

Some schemes and standards require that the carbon offsetting occurs in a country which has not signed up to the Kyoto agreement, and which is an undeveloped country.

The *Consumers' Guide to Retail Offset Providers* by an organisation called Clean Air-Cool Planet provides a more detailed guide to the type of questions which should be asked when purchasing carbon offsets.

Carbon offset standards

There are a growing number of internationally recognised standards which ensure that relevant criteria are met when carbon offsets are purchased. WWF published a comprehensive comparison[73] of the more common offset standards in March 2008. Carbon offset standards include the Gold Standard, the Voluntary Carbon Standard and the DEFRA code.

All three standards need to prove additionality, be independently verified, be used for permanent projects and be unique – only used once and with an assurance that there are no leakage effects.

The Gold Standard does not apply to tree planting projects. It only applies to those offsets which increase energy efficiency and contribute towards the development of sustainable energy. Gold Standard carbon offsets need to be tracked in the Gold Standard Registry, run by APX[74] and meet the UNFCCC's registry protocol. The credits must be permanent, as calculated by UN-approved methodologies in the CDM stream and GS Technical Advisory Committee methodologies in the voluntary stream. The project needs to be located in a country which *does not* have emission reduction targets under the Kyoto Protocol; these are primarily developing countries.

The Voluntary Carbon Standard (VCS) is considered by some to be the most rigorous of the voluntary standards. The VCS manages carbon offsets using a registry operated by the Bank of New York.

The Department for Environment, Food and Rural Affairs (DEFRA) code was launched in February 2008 by the UK Government.[75] It is a voluntary code of best practice for carbon offsetting.

Renewable energy certificates

Consumers of electricity from non-sustainable sources are able to offset this electricity by purchasing electricity offsets or

---

[73] *www.wwf.de/fileadmin/fm-wwf/pdf_neu/A_Comparison_of_Carbon_Offset_Standards_lang.pdf.*
[74] *www.apx.com/environmental/environmental-registries.asp.*
[75] 'DEFRA launches process', Carbon Footprint, *www.carbonfootprint.com/defrabestpractice.html.*

Renewable Energy Certificates (REC). These certificates have the same environmental impact as buying electricity from sustainable sources. They are also known as green tags or Tradable Renewable Certificates (TRCs).[76]

For every unit of electricity generated from a renewable energy project, there is a corresponding REC which can be sold. RECs are measured in kilowatt hours (kWh) or megawatt hours (mWh). The money generated from the sale of RECs goes to finance new and existing renewable energy facilities.

Carbon trading

Carbon trading describes the process of buying and selling carbon credits. They are bought and sold on trading platforms, by international brokers and online retailers. When an individual or organisation subscribes to a carbon offsetting project, they purchase offsets measured in tonnes of CO_2 emission-reduction offsets.

For example, say one individual has a carbon footprint of seven tonnes of CO_2 a year which is based on a range of factors including:

* 10,000 miles a year travelling by car
* 5,000 miles a year rail travel
* £300 ($550) a year spent on electricity
* secondary purchasing choices such as the occasional purchase of organic food, the purchasing of goods from underdeveloped countries and the purchasing of goods having minimal packaging.

They could choose, for example, to sell their car and travel by bicycle or walk. Alternatively, they could choose to enjoy the convenience of using a car and redeem that CO_2 emission cost by purchasing offsets. One online retailer selected quoted a

---

[76] 'Are you Carbon Neutral?' Electronic products, March 2008, *www2.electronicproducts.com/Are_You_Carbon_Neutral--article-FAMS_Carbon_Mar2008-html.aspx.*

price of £50 ($92) to offset seven tonnes of CO_2, with a choice of projects to subscribe to.

Carbon trading can be driven by mandatory and voluntary schemes. The mandatory schemes mainly derive from agreements such as Kyoto, using systems such as the 'cap-and-trade' process. Under a cap-and-trade system, a mandatory cap or minimum allowance of CO_2 emissions is set. This minimum amount, or amount of CO_2 emissions to be reduced, is referred to as the 'allowance'. Some organisations may be given free allowances, perhaps based on their historic CO_2 emissions.

The cap-and-trade system usually applies to countries, regions or larger organisations. The cap is set by regulation and/or taxes, or in the case of countries and regions, by political negotiation.

The process for the cap-and-trade carbon emission reduction process is depicted in the following diagram:

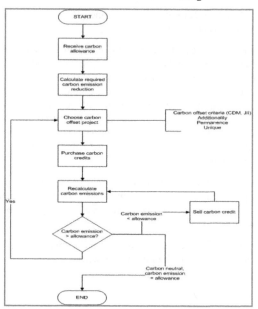

Figure 4: Flowchart depicting the process for the cap-and-trade carbon emission reduction process

Organisations which are mandatorily required to reduce their CO_2 emissions are provided with a CO_2 emission target. They calculate their carbon footprint and from that derive their carbon emission reduction target in tonnes. They choose a carbon offset project which meets the carbon offset criteria under the mandatory scheme. They then purchase carbon credits and recalculate their carbon emission. If this is still above the allowed level, they buy some additional carbon credits from carbon offset projects or from other companies. If this is below the allowed level, the organisation is able to sell carbon credits.

The voluntary market follows a similar process. However, participating organisations are monitored by the voluntary standards. Organisations are reducing their CO_2 emissions voluntarily and do not sell carbon credits.

Carbon trading is market driven in the sense that the price of a carbon offset is set by the market. The market will be influenced by supply and demand – the fewer the number of offsets that are available, the more expensive they will be. Conversely, the greater the number of offsets that are available, the cheaper they will be. Organisations can choose to reduce their CO_2 emissions, or to purchase carbon offsets, whichever is the cheaper. It may be, for example, that it is initially cheaper for an organisation to purchase carbon offsets than to reduce their CO_2 emissions. However, if there is a high demand for carbon offsets and the price goes up there may be a point at which it is cheaper for an organisation to reduce their CO_2 emissions. For this reason, carbon trading is sometimes described as the mechanism which is the most cost-effective way of reducing emissions.

The greatest problems encountered with carbon trading are double counting and an over-allocation of allowances. There have been accusations that the EU ETS scheme has double counted carbon allowances.[77] There have also been accusations of an over-allocation of allowances of millions of UK pounds, with little or no benefit to the environment.[78]

There have been suggestions in the UK of plans to charge individuals for the amount of carbon that they use.[79] However, a source from the organisation Carbon Footprint[80] said that she thought that this was unlikely in the near future.

---

[77] 'EU trading scheme slammed for "double counting" carbon credits'. BusinessGreen, 26 November 2007, *www.businessgreen.com/business-green/news/2204331/emissions-trading-slammed.*
[78] 'Britain's worst polluters set for windfall of millions', 12 September 2008, *www.guardian.co.uk/environment/2008/sep/12/emissionstrading.*
[79] 'Miliband unveils carbon swipe-card plan', 19 July 2006, *The Guardian,*
www.guardian.co.uk/politics/2006/jul/19/greenpolitics.travelnews.
[80] *www.carbonfootprint.com.*

Carbon trading schemes

There is a number of carbon trading schemes:

- The European Union Emissions Trading Scheme (EU ETS)
- The Carbon Reduction Commitment (CRC)
- The Regional Greenhouse Gas Initiative (RGGI), comprised of New York and the New England states, has emissions trading and offsets as part of a compulsory cap-and-trade system for energy generators
- The California Climate Action Registry (CCAR), set up by the State of California, is a voluntary reporting initiative for companies and other organisations, such as municipalities, with plans for targets and trading in the future
- The Chicago Climate Exchange (CCX) is another voluntary registry and trading platform where members take part in a cap-and-trade regime, with allowances and offsets being traded on the CCX.

The European Union Emissions Trading Scheme (EU ETS)

This was the first international trading scheme.[81] It operates using the cap-and-trade process. This scheme is aimed at those organisations within Europe who generate the largest amounts of CO_2 emissions. Under the EU ETS scheme, 10,500 of Europe's biggest polluting firms are assigned carbon allowances.

The EU ETS is policed in the UK by the Environment Agency which contacts involved businesses directly. The type of business required to participate in the scheme is set by the EU guidelines. The scheme is required to be verified by third parties.

---

[81] 'A Guide to U.K. Carbon Trading Schemes', Tom Young, 21 August 2008, *www.climatebiz.com/feature/2008/08/21/a-guide-uk-carbon-trading-schemes*.

The Environment Agency issues permits which require businesses to monitor and report emissions in accordance with the EU guidelines. There are three phases to the scheme, running from 2005–2008, 2008–2012 and 2013 onwards. Tom Young, from Greener Computing describes the success of the first phase:

The first phase of the scheme ran from the beginning of 2005 to the end of 2007. It was widely considered a failure because over-allocation of free allowances led to a huge price crash in 2006. It also emerged that some companies had made millions from the scheme by selling off the credits that they were freely allocated while delivering minimal cuts in emissions.[82]

The second phase has a more controlled allocation of allowances which has generated more stable prices of 'between €20 (£15 or \$29) and €30 (£34 or \$44)) per tonne'. The third phase is expected to include a greater number of industries.

Once a CO_2 emission reduction project has been developed, the project will need to be accredited by the UNFCCC (who negotiated the Kyoto agreement). The project can then be linked to an official emission trading programme such as the EU ETS.[83]

The Exchequer Secretary to the Treasury, Angela Eagle MP, announced in September 2008 that the UK's first auction of carbon trading allowances – under the EU ETS – would be held on 19 November 2008, making the UK the first country in Europe to hold an auction in Phase II of the EU ETS.[84]

---

[82] 'A Guide to U.K. Carbon Trading Schemes', Tom Young, 21 August 2008,
www.climatebiz.com/feature/2008/08/21/a-guide-uk-carbon-trading-schemes.
[83] 'Are you Carbon Neutral?' Electronic products, March 2008,
www2.electronicproducts.com/Are_You_Carbon_Neutral--article-FAMS_Carbon_Mar2008-html.aspx.
[84] HM Treasury, 18 September 2008, *www.hm-treasury.gov.uk/press_95_08.htm*.

The UK's Carbon Reduction Commitment

This is a smaller scale cap-and-trade scheme. This scheme is also policed by the Environment Agency, which requires participants to submit annual statements to them via an online registry. The Environment Agency also audits the scheme. The Carbon Reduction Commitment (CRC) is aimed at organisations which spend more than £500,000 ($930,500 or 623,313 Euros) a year on electricity. The scheme also applies to the UK's schools, hospitals and other public sector bodies.

The UN carbon trading flexibility mechanisms

As part of the Kyoto Protocol, the United Nations (UN) developed three 'flexibility mechanisms' aimed at promoting carbon trading:[85]

Emissions Trading

This mechanism enables Annex I countries, or countries which have a Kyoto obligation to reduce their CO_2 emissions, to trade GHG emissions allowances with each other. Such trading needs to show additionality. Each country retains ultimate responsibility for complying with the Protocol.

Joint Implementation (JI)

This mechanism enables an Annex I country to meet its emissions-reduction target by investing in a project in another Annex I country which reduces GHG emissions. These reductions are also required to provide additionality.

Clean Development Mechanism (CDM)

The CDM enables companies in Annex I countries to invest in projects in the developing world to reduce GHGs. These

---

[85] 'Kyoto Protocol: Trade versus the environment', Helen Loose, *Energy & Environment*, Vol. 12, No. 1, 2001.

reductions again require proof of additionality.[86] The CDM mechanism issues CERs, which are tradable units. Each CER represents one metric tonne of carbon emissions reduction.

---

[86] 'Meeting the Challenge', David Suzuki Foundation, 2007.

ITG RESOURCES

IT Governance Ltd source, create and deliver products and services to meet the real-world, evolving IT governance needs of today's organisations, directors, managers and practitioners. The ITG website (*www.itgovernance.co.uk*) is the international one-stop-shop for corporate and IT governance information, advice, guidance, books, tools, training and consultancy.

www.itgovernance.co.uk/green-it.aspx is the ITG website that includes a comprehensive range of books, tools, project templates, resources and links for Green IT and ISO14001.

Pocket Guides

For full details of the entire range of pocket guides, simply follow the links at *www.itgovernance.co.uk/publishing.aspx*. The current range includes the following companions to this guide:

The Green Office: *www.itgovernance.co.uk/products/2200*

The Green Agenda: a Business Guide
www.itgovernance.co.uk/products/2202

The Governance of Green IT
www.itgovernance.co.uk/products/2106

Toolkits

ITG's unique range of toolkits includes *The Green IT Implementation Toolkit*, which contains all the tools and guidance that you will need in order to develop and implement an appropriate Green IT action plan for your organisation. Full details can be found at *www.itgovernance.co.uk/products/2201*.

Best Practice Reports

ITG's new range of Best Practice Reports is now at *www.itgovernance.co.uk/best-practice-reports.aspx*. These offer you essential, pertinent, expertly researched information on an increasing number of key issues, including Green IT.

Training and Consultancy

IT Governance also offer training and consultancy services across the entire spectrum of disciplines in the information governance arena. Details of training courses can be accessed at *www.itgovernance.co.uk/training.aspx* and descriptions of our consultancy services can be found at *http://www.itgovernance.co.uk/consulting.aspx*.

Why not contact us to see how we could help you and your organisation?

Newsletter

IT governance is one of the hottest topics in business today, not least because it is also the fastest moving, so what better way to keep up than by subscribing to ITG's free monthly newsletter *Sentinel*? It provides monthly updates and resources across the whole spectrum of IT governance subject matter, including risk management, information security, ITIL and IT service management, project governance, compliance and so much more. Subscribe for your free copy at: *www.itgovernance.co.uk/newsletter.aspx*.

Printed by BoD™in Norderstedt, Germany